BASKETBALL

CHRISTINA LEMKE

Rourke
Educational Media

rourkeeducationalmedia.com

Guided Reading Level: O

Scan for Related Titles and Teacher Resources

TABLE OF CONTENTS

GET PSYCHED!

Jump ball! The ref throws the ball into the air. You grab it! You **dribble** the ball down the court, spinning around.

You shoot. The ball swooshes through the net. Score! Your team won the game! You are psyched to play basketball!

GAME ON!

Cutting the Net: In 1922, high school basketball coach Everett Case began cutting the net off the hoop each time his team won the state championship as a keepsake. When he became the coach at North Carolina State University and his team won the 1946 Southern Conference title, his players hoisted him up so he could cut the net once again.

GAME ON

Basketball is a popular team sport. It is played by people all over the world.

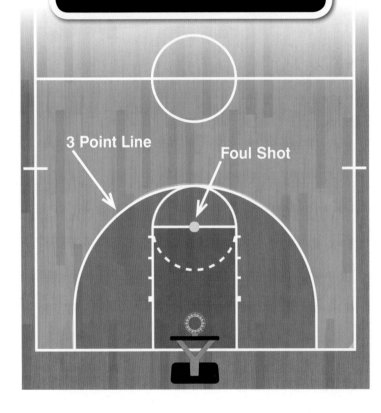

GAME ON!

SCORE!
- 3 points behind the 3-point line
- 2 points inside the 3-point line
- 1 point foul shot

3 Point Line

Foul Shot

To score points, players on the offense try to throw the basketball into the net. Watch out for the defense! They try to take away the ball or block shots.

Defense

Offense

Each team has five players on the court. The court is a rectangle that is 94 feet (28.7 meters) long and 50 feet (15.2 meters) wide.

94 feet

50 feet

Do the Math: What is the area of a basketball court? (Answer: Area 94 x 50 = 4,700 square feet (1,432.6 square meters)

GAME ON!
The Harlem Globetrotters have been entertaining crowds around the world with their unique basketball tricks and comedic routines for almost 100 years. They were the first team to play basketball in Europe. They have played for popes, kings, queens, and presidents.

At each end of the court is a basket. It is ten feet (three meters) high. Sometimes players will bounce the ball against the **backboard** to get shots into the basket. Some players jump high to slam the ball into the net. Slam dunk!

10 Feet

Jump ball! To begin the game, the official throws the ball straight up into the air. One player from each team jumps up, hitting the ball to a teammate. The team that gets the ball is on the offense.

GAME ON!

In the early days of basketball, a jump ball in the center of the court followed each basket.

Carrying the ball down the court would be too easy. Players have to dribble the ball as they move down the court. A player that stops dribbling has to shoot or pass the ball.

GAME ON!

When a player breaks a rule, it is called a foul. A defender pushing an offensive player that's shooting the ball is the most common foul.

SUIT UP!

  With all that running back and forth, your clothes need to be comfortable. Basketball shirts have no sleeves. The shorts are loose-fitting.

Basketball players on recreational and professional teams wear uniforms. The jerseys and shirts use at least two colors. Teams have uniforms for playing at home and playing away.

GAME ON!

For some games, special clothing designers create unique designs. For the National Basketball Association (NBA) games played on December 25, 2015, players wore socks that looked like Christmas sweaters with their special Christmas Day uniforms.

Many players also wear special sneakers called high-tops. They are made to prevent players from getting hurt.

GAME ON!

The first basketball sneaker was released in 1917 by Converse. Three years later, basketball star Chuck Taylor loaned his name to these new shoes. Now, "Chuck Taylors" are worn not only by basketball players, but also rockers, skaters, and other fashionistas.

These shoes protect the ankle better than regular sneakers. They lace up to the top. They also have bottoms that do not skid on the court.

GAME ON!

The most expensive basketball sneakers are a version of Nike's Jordan I. Only 12 pairs of the black and metallic gold version were released in Asia. A pair will cost you $25,000!

What do you do when it's way too cold outside and your students are wild? Invent a game! YMCA physical education teacher Dr. James Naismith invented the game of basketball in 1891.

Dr. James Naismith 1861–1939

YMCA boys basketball team in 1919

GAME ON!

Dr. Naismith wrote the 13 original rules of basketball. He hung them on a wall in the gymnasium.

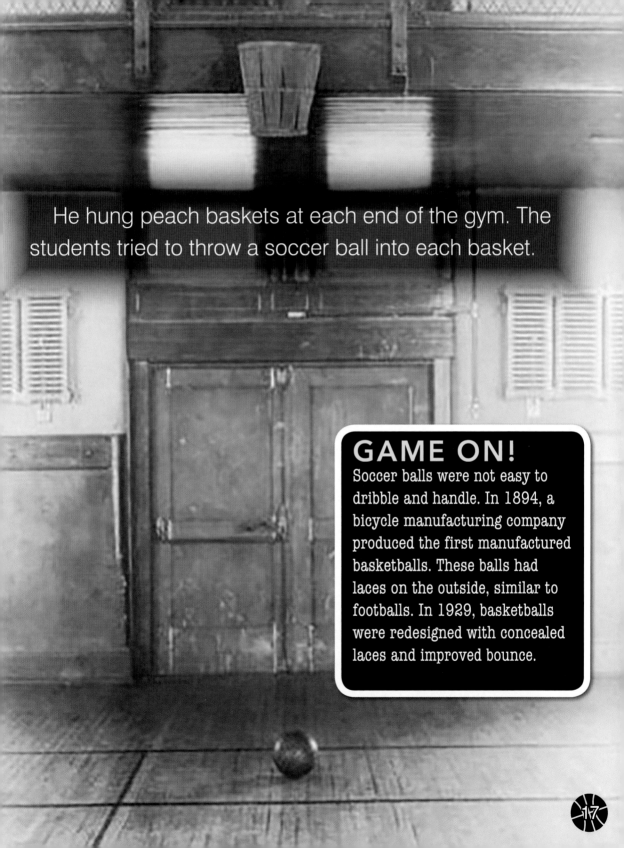

He hung peach baskets at each end of the gym. The students tried to throw a soccer ball into each basket.

GAME ON!

Soccer balls were not easy to dribble and handle. In 1894, a bicycle manufacturing company produced the first manufactured basketballs. These balls had laces on the outside, similar to footballs. In 1929, basketballs were redesigned with concealed laces and improved bounce.

The National Basketball Association (NBA) is a professional league formed for male players in 1949. There are 30 teams in cities throughout the United States.

- O Seattle SuperSonics
- O Portland Trail Blazers
- Minnesota Timberwolves (Minneapolis) O
- Milwaukee Bucks O
- Detroit Pistons O
- Toronto Raptors O
- Boston Celtics O
- Utah Jazz O (Salt Lake City)
- Chicago Bulls O
- New Jersey Nets O
- New York Knicks O
- Sacramento Kings O O
- O Denver Nuggets
- Cleveland Cavaliers O
- Philadelphia 76ers O
- Golden State Warriors (Oakland)
- Indiana Pacers O (Indianapolis)
- Washington Wizards
- Los Angeles Clippers
- O Los Angeles Lakers
- Memphis Grizzlies O
- O Charlotte Bobcats
- Phoenix Suns O
- Atlanta Hawks O
- Dallas Mavericks O
- New Orleans Hornets O
- San Antonio Spurs O
- Houston Rockets O
- Orlando Magic O
- Miami Heat O

WESTERN CONFERENCE
O NORTHWEST DIVISION
O PACIFIC DIVISION
O SOUTHWEST DIVISION

EASTERN CONFERENCE
O ATLANTIC DIVISION
O CENTRAL DIVISION
O SOUTHEAST DIVISION

N
500 km
300 mi

GAME ON!

The New York Knicks and the Boston Celtics are the only two teams in the original NBA that still exist. The other teams either folded or moved to different cities.

In 1996, the Women's National Basketball Association (WNBA) was created. There are 12 teams in this professional league that boasts the best female players. Go, girls!

GAME ON!

In 1892, college gymnastics teacher Senda Berenson read about Naismith's game. Since women were not allowed to take part in strenuous activity at that time, Berenson changed the rules so her classes could play this new sport.

Do the Math:
How many years after the NBA was the WNBA created?
(Answer: 1996-1949 = 47)

19

SCIENCE OF BASKETBALL

Did you know science is part of basketball? Players use **physics** for the perfect 3-point shot. The ball needs to fly with the right speed and the right bend.

The ball needs an arc of 45 degrees, a speed of just under 20 miles (32 kilometers) per hour, and two revolutions per second of spin.

Your hands have super powers! A player's hands give the ball energy to make it bounce. The bounce of the ball is called **kinetic energy**.

GAME ON!

Free Throw Like a Pro: Look at the basket. Shoot with your dominant hand and use the other hand to balance the ball. Release the ball from your fingertips to get a good rotation.

Basketball shoes have **evolved** to help players run faster and jump higher. Scientists create special materials to make the shoes better.

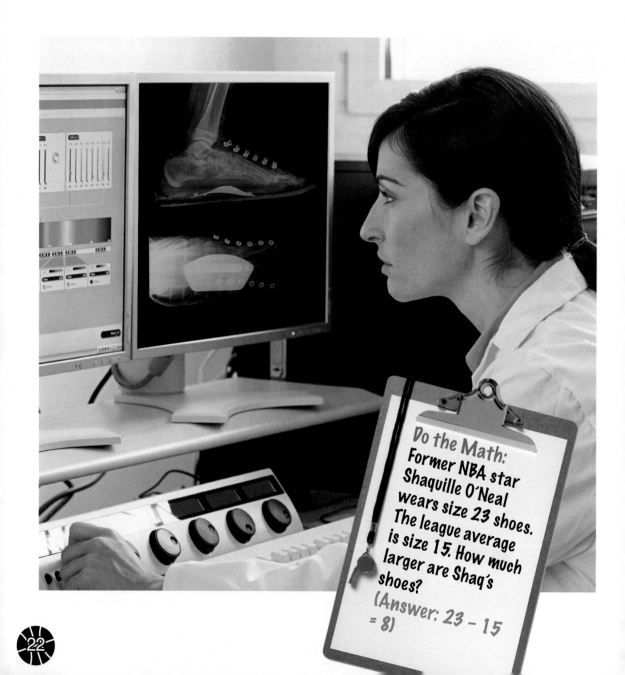

Do the Math:
Former NBA star Shaquille O'Neal wears size 23 shoes. The league average is size 15. How much larger are Shaq's shoes?
(Answer: 23 – 15 = 8)

Computers are used to help players **analyze** how they move. Coaches use this information to make training plans to help the players be stronger and move faster.

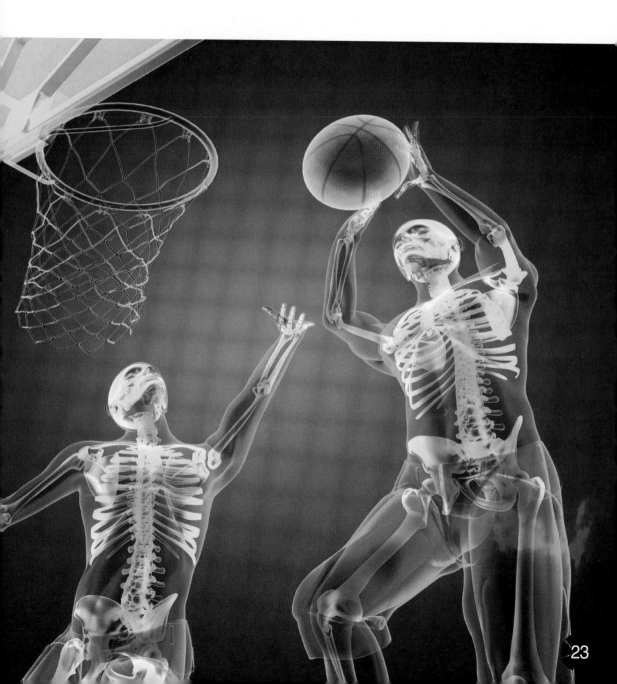

AROUND THE WORLD

Since its invention in the U.S. by a Canadian gym teacher, basketball has become a global sport. The first game played in Europe was in 1893 at a YMCA in Paris, France.

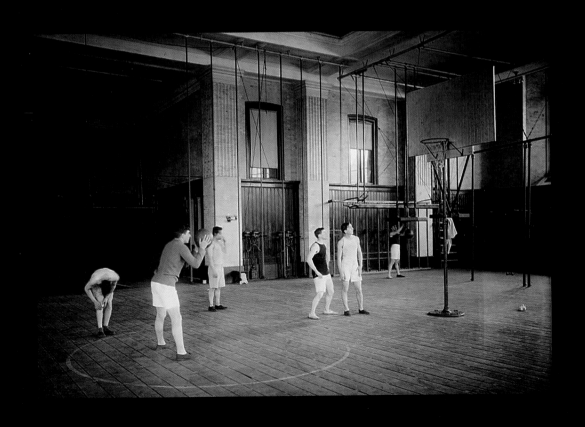

Basketball Euroleague - Cedevita Zagreb vs. Lokomotiv Kuban Krasnodar in Croatia

Basketball has become so popular in Europe that a competition called the Euroleague was created. Twenty-four teams from throughout Europe play through a season until one team is the champion. It is the second largest competition in the world, after the NBA.

The country with the largest number of people also loves basketball! YMCA **missionaries** from the United States brought the game to China in 1895. Chinese national Yao Ming was drafted by the Houston Rockets in 2002. That same year, the NBA China division was created in Beijing, China.

Yao Ming, formerly of the Houston Rockets

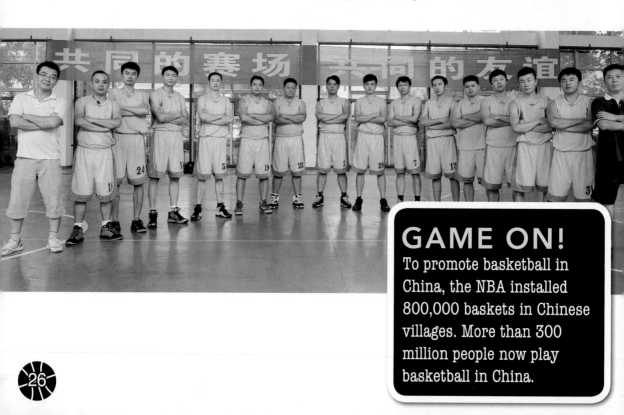

GAME ON!

To promote basketball in China, the NBA installed 800,000 baskets in Chinese villages. More than 300 million people now play basketball in China.

Basketball is gaining popularity in India. The NBA has hosted over 450 grassroots events in ten Indian cities since 2008. They also created a recreational league with 6,000 players.

Recreational basketball court in India

GAME ON!

In 2015, Satnam Singh became the first Indian player drafted into the NBA. He was chosen by the Dallas Mavericks.

READY TO PLAY?

There's more to being a basketball player than what happens on the court. Athletes keep their bodies in top shape by eating healthy foods, such as lean protein, fruits, and vegetables.

It is also important to drink water before, during, and after practice to stay **hydrated**.

GAME ON!

Giving Back: LeBron James is one of the most charitable players in the NBA. Most recently, his foundation donated 41 million dollars to send 1,100 kids to the University of Akron, the community he grew up in.

Athletes are expected to respect their coaches, teammates, and **opponents**. They can be role models on and off the court.

So what do you think? Are you psyched to play basketball?

GAME ON!

"I've missed more than 9,000 shots in my career. I've lost almost 300 games. 26 times, I've been trusted to take the game winning shot and missed. I've failed over and over again in my life. And that is why I succeed."
—NBA legend Michael Jordan

Coach's notes:
- Arrive at practice on time
- Eat a healthy meal before practice
- Get enough sleep
- Do your best on and off the court
- Respect everyone

GLOSSARY

analyze (AH-nu-lize): to study something in a careful manner

backboard (BAHK-bord): the rectangular board behind the basket on a basketball court

dribble (DRIH-buhl): bouncing a ball quickly on the ground

evolved (ee-VOL-vd): changed over time to become better

kinetic energy (kih-NEH-tihk EHN-er-jee): energy with movement

hydrated (HYE-dray-tihd): having the proper amount of water in the body

missionaries (MIH-shun-air-eez): a group of people who engage in charitable work with religious support

opponents (op-POH-nents): players on a team competing against another team in a game

physics (FIH-zihks): the scientific study of matter and energy

INDEX

SHOW WHAT YOU KNOW

1. What is the job of the defense?
2. Who invented the game of basketball?
3. How is physics important in basketball?
4. What countries have professional basketball leagues?
5. Who introduced basketball to China?

WEBSITES TO VISIT

www.sciencebuddies.org

www.wnba.com

www.usab.com/youth

ABOUT THE AUTHOR

Christina Lemke lives in Florida with her husband and son. She enjoys cheering on her son when he plays all kinds of sports, including soccer and baseball. She loves to relax by reading at the beach. Her favorite basketball teams are the Miami Heat and the New York Liberty.

Meet The Author!
www.meetREMauthors.com

www.rourkeeducationalmedia.com

PHOTO CREDITS: Cover, title page: ©Aksonov; p.3: ©2010-JaniBryson; p.4: ©eurobanks; p.4, 5, 7, 10, 12-13: ©Christopher Futcher; p.5, 14: ©skynesher; p.6: ©enterlinedesign, ©pedalist; p.8: ©Tequilaslam; p.10: ©Aspen Photo; p.11: ©DNY59; p.14, 16, 17: Public Domain; p.15: ©franckreporter, ©Alexey_R; p.16, 24: Library of Congress; p.19: ©Photo Works; p.20: ©Costasz; p.21: ©andresr; p.22: ©Image Source; p.23: ©video-doctor; p.24: ©Barnaby Chambers; p.25: ©jpgfactory, ©krumcek; p.26: Wikipedia, ©Mengtianhan; p.27: ©thorgal67, ©Zoran Ivanovic Photography; p.28: ©Steve Debenport, ©A.RICARDO; p.29: ©Steve Lipofsky, ©moneybusinessimages

Edited by: Keli Sipperley

Cover and interior design by: Rhea Magaro

Library of Congress PCN Data

Basketball / Christina Lemke
(Game On! Psyched For Sports)
ISBN (hard cover)(alk. paper) 978-1-68191-756-6
ISBN (soft cover) 978-1-68191-857-0
ISBN (e-Book) 978-1-68191-947-8
Library of Congress Control Number: 2016932718

Also Available as:

ROURKE'S
e-Books